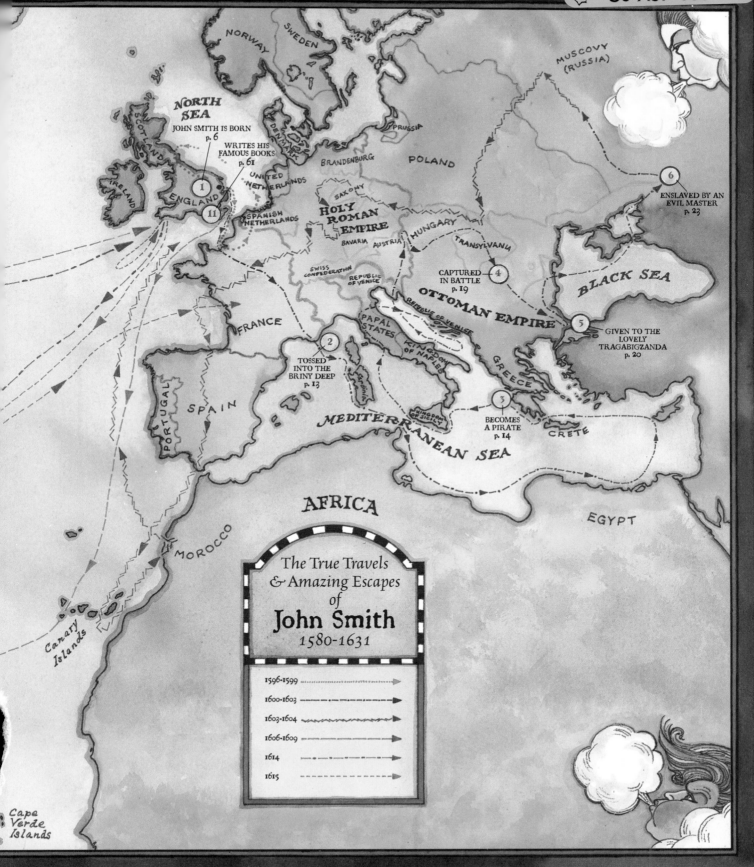

NORTH
SEA

NORWAY

SWEDEN

DENMARK

MUSCOVY
(RUSSIA)

PRUSSIA

POLAND

SCOTLAND

IRELAND

ENGLAND

JOHN SMITH IS BORN
p. 6

WRITES HIS
FAMOUS BOOKS
p. 61

UNITED
NETHERLANDS

SPANISH
NETHERLANDS

BRANDENBURG

SAXONY

HOLY
ROMAN
EMPIRE

BAVARIA   AUSTRIA

HUNGARY

TRANSYLVANIA

⑥
ENSLAVED BY AN
EVIL MASTER
p. 23

SWISS
CONFEDERATION

REPUBLIC
OF VENICE

④
CAPTURED
IN BATTLE
p. 19

BLACK SEA

FRANCE

PAPAL
STATES

REPUBLIC OF VENICE

OTTOMAN EMPIRE

⑤
GIVEN TO THE
LOVELY
TRAGABIGZANDA
p. 20

KINGDOM
OF NAPLES

②
TOSSED
INTO THE
BRINY DEEP
p. 13

PORTUGAL

SPAIN

SARDINIA

GREECE

CRETE

KINGDOM OF SICILY

③
BECOMES
A PIRATE
p. 14

MEDITERRANEAN SEA

AFRICA

EGYPT

MOROCCO

Canary
Islands

The True Travels
& Amazing Escapes
of
John Smith
1580-1631

1596-1599
1600-1603
1603-1604
1606-1609
1614
1615

Cape
Verde
Islands

John Smith Escapes Again!

BY ROSALYN SCHANZER

NATIONAL GEOGRAPHIC

Washington, D.C.

For Adam & Stacey

Printed in the United States

Book design by David M. Seager
The body text is set in Caslon Antique
The display text is set in 1722 Roman

Library of Congress
Cataloging-in-Publication Information
is available from the
Library of Congress upon request.

Trade ISBN 10: 0-7922-5930-0
Trade ISBN 13: 978-0-7922-5930-5
Library Binding ISBN 10: 0-7922-5931-9
Library Binding ISBN 13: 978-0-7922-5931-2

For information about special discounts for bulk purchases,
please contact National Geographic Books Special Sales:
ngspecsales@ngs.org

One of the world's largest nonprofit scientific and educational
organizations, the National Geographic Society was founded in
1888 "for the increase and diffusion of geographic knowledge."
Fulfilling this mission, the Society educates and inspires millions
every day through its magazines, books, television programs,
videos, maps and atlases, research grants, the National Geographic
Bee, teacher workshops, and innovative classroom materials.
The Society is supported through membership dues, charitable
gifts, and income from the sale of its educational products. This
support is vital to National Geographic's mission to increase global
understanding and promote conservation of our planet through
exploration, research, and education.

NATIONAL GEOGRAPHIC SOCIETY
1145 17th Street N.W.
Washington, D.C. 20036-4688 U.S.A.

Visit the Society's Web site: www.nationalgeographic.com

Foreword

If you've ever heard of John Smith, the only thing you probably remember is that he was rescued from sure and certain death by Pocahontas, a beautiful American Indian girl. But did you know that John Smith was America's first genuine superstar? At one time or another, this swashbuckling Englishman was a heroic warrior who won battles against impossible odds, a daring world explorer, a president, a mapmaker, a peacekeeper, and the author whose books jumpstarted the Great American Dream of a better life for ordinary people.

And here's the biggest surprise. In his day, John Smith was probably the greatest escape artist on the planet. He escaped from danger over and over, and not only from Indians, but from angry mobs, slave drivers, French pirates, and even the deep blue sea.

How did he do that? To find the answer, let's take a look at a few of the escape stories John told in his very own books (and while we're at it, we can check out some of his famous adventures, too).* But first, we'll set the scene...

*For more on John Smith's point of view as revealed in this book, see the Author's Note, pages 62-63.

Introduction

The Scene Is Set

Olde England was the place to be in 1580. Elizabeth I, nicknamed "Good Queen Bess" by her adoring subjects, was busy ruling over England's glorious Golden Age. Pirate-explorer Francis Drake sailed home after a three-year voyage all the way around the world. Young William Shakespeare had just turned 16. Wealthy men and women wearing jewel-covered costumes rode off to balls in fancy carriages, while knights in glittering armor rode off to battle on prancing steeds. And in a featherbed on a farm in the tiny village of Willoughby, a baby boy was born who would change the future of a new and far-off world. His name, of course, was John Smith. What a life this baby would lead!

About 1586 to 1595 (Ages 6–15)

John went to two free schools. He studied Latin grammar, morality, good manners, and religion (but he would much rather have learned to be a sailor).

1595 (Age 15)

John became the apprentice of a wealthy merchant named Thomas Sendall. He learned to do bookkeeping (but would still rather have gone to sea).

1596 (Age 16)

John's father died and left him 7 acres of land, 3 orchards, and some livestock. John ESCAPED from his boring apprenticeship by selling the livestock and setting out at once to see the world.

1596 or 1597 to 1599 (Ages 16–19)

John joined many other Englishmen as a volunteer soldier in the Netherlands. They were helping to fight for the Dutch Protestants' independence from Catholic Spain.

1599 (Age 19)

John traveled through France and visited the glamorous city of Paris. He was badly hurt in a terrible shipwreck on his way to Scotland. Once he recovered, he tried but failed to get a job in the court of the Scottish king. Even so, by now he was hooked on adventure for life.

Perhaps late 1599 through summer 1600 (Ages 19–20)

John returned to England and camped out in the countryside, where he practiced jousting and read scholarly books about the art of war. His goal: To become an officer in the Austrian army and fight the dreaded Turks, who were trying to take over Europe.

Winter 1600 (Age 20)

On his way to join the army, John met four scoundrels posing as gentlemen. They offered to sail with him to France, where they would introduce him to the general in charge of fighting the Turks. It was a dirty trick. The scoundrels soon snuck ashore with all of John's fine clothes and money, and he had to sell his winter cloak to pay for passage.

Our Hero Is Tossed into the Briny Deep and Becomes a Pirate

John had a long way to go if he aimed to catch up with the Austrian Army and fight the Turks. Once his ship landed in northern France, he spent a freezing winter hitchhiking south and relying on the kindness of strangers for food and warm clothes. By spring, he had finally reached the port town of Marseille, where he got aboard yet another ship and headed off toward Italy.*

John's fellow passengers turned out to be a collection of country bumpkins and Catholic pilgrims from many nations traveling to Rome. Whoops. As you might remember, John Smith and lots of other Englishmen had recently fought for a Protestant Army in a big war against the Catholics. There was still bad blood between Catholics and Protestants, and John was the only Protestant on board.

Before very long, a powerful spring storm churned the sea into froth. The wind and waves got so intense that the ship set anchor behind a little island to keep out of harm's way. It didn't help. Rain kept pouring down in torrents, and the winds howled on.

* Look at the map on the endpapers to follow John Smith's journeys and escape routes all over the world.

Everyone was scared to death. The Catholic pilgrims were sure this furious storm was a punishment from God because an English Protestant had been allowed on board. The superstitious country bumpkins agreed. The angry mob began to curse at John. They swore that all Englishmen were pirates. They screamed that Queen Elizabeth was a Protestant monster. Growing wilder by the minute, they yelled that the seas would never calm down again as long as John was on the ship! They were so enraged that they threw him overboard, smack dab into the stormy sea.

John dodged the crashing waves and swam through the storm as hard as he could. At long last, he reached the little island. Night was coming on, and he must have been terribly cold and hungry. What's worse, he was trapped in the middle of nowhere with no dry clothes, food, or shelter. The only living things on the island were a few wild goats and cows. He may have escaped from drowning, but how would he ever escape from this deserted place?

By the next day, John's ship was long gone, but he spotted a couple of other ships at anchor. They had been trying to avoid the storm, too! Once he flagged them down, a French captain fetched John on board and gave him dry clothes and something to eat. In fact, the crew was so friendly that John cheerfully delayed his plans to become a soldier and decided to try his fortune with the sailors. This was the fastest and easiest escape he would have in his whole life. It also turned out to be the luckiest.

The ship set out on a long voyage that followed the coast of Africa, continued past Egypt, Cyprus, and Greece, and headed toward Italy. One day, the French captain hailed a big merchant vessel from Venice. The vessel replied in a most unfriendly way: It fired its cannons at the French ship, killing a sailor. The French captain was so mad that he fired back with every weapon on board. This destroyed the Venetian's sails, so they set the French ship on fire.

John and his friends were infuriated. They fought harder than ever and finally won the battle. They put out their fires, patched their leaks, chained their prisoners—and rifled the other ship, unloading a fabulous haul of fine silks, plush velvets, fancy golden cloth, and sparkling gold and silver coins. Then they set the enemy vessel free along with its crew. You might say that John and all his new friends were now pirates. Pirate John Smith went ashore at Antibes in southern France with five hundred gold coins and a very valuable little treasure box.

SPANISH NETHERLANDS

HOLY ROMAN EMPIRE

POLAND

BAVARIA

AUSTRIA

Danube River

HUNGARY

MOLDAVIA

SWISS CONFEDERATION

Graz

2

3

4

Alba Regalis

Olumpagh

TRANSYLVANIA

Alba Julia

5

FRANCE

REPUBLIC OF VENICE

Venice

1

TRANSYLVANIAN ALPS

Antibes

PAPAL STATES

ADRIATIC SEA

REP. OF VENICE

Drava River

OTTOMAN EMPIRE

WALLACHIA

TUSCANY

1

Danube River

CORSICA

Rome

1

KINGDOM OF NAPLES

SARDINIA

Naples

AFRICA

KINGDOM OF SICILY

Cephalonia

GREECE

MEDITERRANEAN SEA

W

N

E

S

CRETE

Spring 1601 (Age 21)

Summer 1601

Next, John headed for Graz, an Austrian town in the Holy Roman Empire, where he finally joined a small regiment of the Austrian army and set off to fight the Turks.

Summer 1601

Turkish forces had surrounded a Hungarian town, cutting it off from all hope. John taught his general how to get coded messages to and from the townsfolk. To help set them free, he set off a string of fireworks that fooled the Turks into thinking that thousands of Austrian guns were firing at them. Instead of charging the real Austrian army, Turkish forces charged the fireworks by mistake. The army joined the townsfolk to ambush the Turks from behind and free the town. John had made quite a name for himself. He was promoted to be the captain of 250 horsemen.

From France, John traveled to Tuscany, Rome, Naples, and Venice. He used his newly won riches to go sightseeing all over the region in the style of a gentleman.

Fall 1601

To help win a Turkish fortress, John invented some special weapons he called "Fiery Dragons." First, 40 or 50 round pots were filled with all kinds of explosives. At midnight, the pots were set afire and catapulted in flaming arcs into the camp of the sleeping Turks, where they blew up!

Spring 1602 (Age 22)

TURKISH LORD   JOHN SMITH

During the siege of a strong Transylvanian town, John fought three single-handed duels to the death on horseback with three Turkish champions. He won each battle by taking the Turks' heads. John was now a legendary hero. He was richly rewarded and promoted to the rank of major. Then the prince of Transylvania named him an English Gentleman.

Escape Number Two

John Becomes a Wretched Slave

Although John's bravery and brilliant tactics had made him a superstar in the Austrian army, his luck was soon to change. One dark November night, several thousand enemy soldiers trapped the Austrians in some woods. Quick as a flash, John thought up a way to help the soldiers escape. He showed them how to attach hundreds of fiery devices to their lance tips. Then they mounted their horses and charged straight through the enemy troops with their lances all ablaze. The plan worked!

The Austrians had almost reached safety, but at the crack of dawn, as many as 40,000 Tartars gathered from all over the countryside and swooped down on them. Vastly outnumbered, John and his army were trapped in the deep, narrow valley of Veristhorne with towering mountains on one side and a rushing river on the other. Both sides battled so fiercely that before long, 30,000 men lay cut and mangled on the ground. Badly wounded, John was discovered by some scavengers who were robbing the dead. When they saw that he was dressed as an officer, they decided they could make lots of money by selling him as a slave.

This time John could not escape so easily. The robbers took their prisoner to a market town, where all the captives were prodded and poked like beasts by anyone who might want to buy them. A Turkish Captain made John wrestle with another slave to test his strength and then bought him to send to his lady love as a present. Finally, the newly sold slaves were chained to each other by their necks and forced to march over 200 miles to Constantinople.*

At first John got lucky. His new mistress turned out to be the beautiful Charatza Tragabigzanda, a Greek girl of noble birth. She was soon crazy about John and forgot all about her old suitor. Charatza never made John do the work of a slave. But because she was still young and lived in her family's home, she worried that her mother might sell this new friend.

John and Charatza could both speak Italian, so they talked to each other in secret. To keep him safe, she made plans to send John to her older brother on the far side of the Black Sea. She also sent along a letter asking the brother to treat John kindly and to teach him the language and customs of the Turks. She hoped that John would return to her when she came of age and could do as she pleased.

*Today's Istanbul in Turkey

After traveling for hundreds of miles by land and sea, John was taken to Nalbrits, where there lay a vast military estate surrounded by high stone walls. Charatza's brother, the official in charge, ruled the countryside from a great stony castle filled with weapons. He turned out to be a monstrous tyrant named Tymor Bashaw who owned hundreds of Christian, Turkish, and North African slaves. All of them were chained, beaten, starved, worked to death, and treated worse than dogs. Not a single one had ever escaped.

The evil brother could read between the lines of his sister's letter. He was furious that she might be in love with an enemy Christian slave. He had his servant strip away all of John's clothes and shave his head and beard. Then he forced John to wear a smelly, itchy hair coat, bolted a heavy iron ring around his neck, and made him the lowliest slave of them all.

John labored for many hard months in this terrible place. One day during the harvest season of 1603, the brother rode his horse into a field where John was threshing grain. For no reason at all, he began to curse at John and beat him mercilessly.

Enough was enough. If he couldn't escape now, John might soon die as a slave. Losing all reason, he smashed the tyrant in the head with his threshing bat and killed him. Then he hid the body under some straw, put on the tyrant's clothes, filled a knapsack with grain, mounted the horse, and galloped away. He was free!

Or was he? Now John was lost without maps or water in the rugged Circassian Desert. Could he escape from this hostile territory as well? Which way should he go? After wandering for two or three days, John spotted a crossroad with a signpost that pointed in many directions. A caravan route headed toward Russia seemed most likely to lead away from his enemies, so off he rode.

Afraid that someone would spot his iron collar and return him to slavery, John flew like the wind for 16 days. At long last, he arrived at a Russian outpost called Aecopolis. Upon hearing about John's escape, the governor took off the terrible iron ring around his neck and treated him so kindly that John wrote "he thought himselfe new risen from death." With great joy, our bold escape artist journeyed far and wide through many different countries. At last, he boarded a French man-of-war in Marrakech. But the crew turned out to be pirates who got into a deadly battle with two Spanish pirate ships! That was when John Smith decided he was sick of wars, slavery, and attacks at sea. He had far nobler adventures in mind.

April 1606 (Age 26)

After more than 100 years of English failures, the Virginia Company of London was formed to take another stab at founding a colony in America. John Smith enthusiastically signed up to go.

December 1606

Some 105 colonists and 39 crewmen crowded themselves onto three tiny ships and sailed toward Virginia in America. About half of the passengers were highborn gentlemen who believed they were way too important to do any work. Most people joined to find gold and a shortcut to the riches of the Orient. But John hoped to explore this new world and help set up its first successful English colony.

During the voyage

Highborn gentleman Edward-Maria Wingfield hated lowborn John Smith and envied his popular tales of adventure. Wingfield jailed John on false charges of plotting to mutiny, murder the council, and declare himself king. On the island of Nevis, a gallows was built to hang John Smith. He wrote sarcastically that he could not be persuaded to use it.

April 26, 1607 (Age 27)

The 3 ships made landfall in the Chesapeake Bay. Unaware that they were on Indian hunting grounds, 20 or 30 men went ashore to take a look around. Some Indians spotted these strange-looking intruders. They wounded 2 men but left when their arrows ran out. Then a secret list of 7 men picked to run the colony was opened and read for the first time. John's name was included! But he was still a prisoner in the ship; certain noblemen would not allow this lowborn farmer's son to become a leader.

May 14, 1607

The new colony of Jamestown was founded on a marshy peninsula up the James River. John's enemy, Edward-Maria Wingfield, was chosen to be president. After 13 weeks of imprisonment, John was finally allowed to come ashore to work, but he was not allowed to sit on the ruling council.

Early Summer 1607

President Wingfield refused to build a fort or unpack any guns because he didn't want to offend the Indians. John predicted that the Indians would attack if the colonists looked weak. He was right: Indians wounded 17 men and killed 2 more. At last, John was invited to join the ruling council. But so many gentlemen thought they were too good to do any work that by the end of June, nearly half the colonists were dead from disease and starvation.

Escape Number Three

John Smith
Is Saved by a Compass

The new American colony was in real trouble. There was nothing left to eat but watery barley and wormy wheat. The men still lived in tents. Swarms of mosquitoes from the marsh were making everyone sick, and slimy salty drinking water made them even sicker. The colonists fired President Wingfield for hiding all the remaining food for himself while everyone starved. But Wingfield's replacement, John Ratcliffe, turned out to be worthless as a leader. He did one thing right, though. He appointed John

Smith to manage all things out of doors and to trade with the Indians.

Working harder than anyone else, John soon set everyone to building new houses. He also traveled to Indian territory to trade for food. Nearby Indians thought the settlers were a bunch of weaklings, but John earned their respect by making the colonists appear much stronger than they really were. Before long, he was able to trade beads, copper, and hatchets for great heaps of the Indians' corn, fish, oysters, venison, turkeys, wild geese, and bread.

Now that John had provided food to eat, the lazy gentlemen began to mutter that he was dragging his feet about looking for a shortcut to the Pacific Ocean, so they gave him another job. In December, John and nine other colonists boarded a boat and set out to explore the Chickahominy River.

After 50 miles, the river got too shallow for the big boat. John anchored outside of arrow range and commanded seven men to stay on board no matter what. Then he took two crew members, hiked upstream, and hired two Indians with canoes as guides. The explorers paddled about 12 miles and stopped to hunt for food.

Meanwhile, John's crew back on the big boat ignored their orders and went ashore. Suddenly, a band of warriors leaped out of the woods and captured one of the men. They tortured him horribly to find out what John was doing in their territory. Then they burned the man alive and raced upriver to find John Smith.

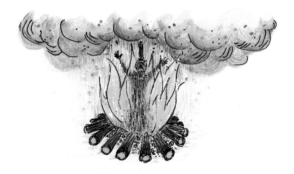

John had no idea that anyone was on his trail. He and a guide were off shooting geese for dinner when they heard hollering coming from their camp. John's friends had just been killed! In a flash, hundreds of warriors headed straight toward John, firing their bows as they ran. An arrow grazed his thigh. He held the guide in front of his body like a shield and shot three attackers with his pistol.

Backing away without looking behind him, John accidentally slid into an ice-cold creek. He was mired in mud and freezing to death, but the Indians, afraid of his pistol, wouldn't come near him. He threw the pistol away, let himself be captured, and hoped for the best.

John Smith was led to a tall, muscular old Indian named
Opechancanough, who was chief of an Indian town named Pamunkee.
If John wanted to escape alive, he would have to use his wits, and fast.
Fearlessly and with great dignity, he reached into his pocket, pulled out
a fancy globe-shaped compass made of ivory and glass, and presented it
to the chief as a gift. Opechancanough had never seen glass before. He
was awestruck. The shiny compass sparkled like a jewel, and the needle
on its fancy round card, trapped inside clear glass, spun around and
around but could never be touched!

Smith had already picked up a little bit of the Indians' language.
Making the most of his flair for storytelling, he used his globe-like
compass to show that the Earth is round, and he explained how the sun
forever chases the night around the world. Then he spun many tales
about other nations whose people have different customs and different
colors of skin.

The Pamunkee Indians were fascinated. Maybe John Smith was some kind of god! But was he dangerous? They tied their prisoner to a tree and prepared to shoot. It looked like he would not escape from death after all.

Just in time, Opechancanough raised the sparkling compass high over John's head. Everyone laid their bows and arrows on the ground. Then Opechancanough made another grand gesture, and with a noisy yell, the warriors untied John from the tree. Was he finally safe? Not exactly.

The Indians triumphantly paraded their captive to a small hunting village, their arrows at the ready. Throngs of women and children stared at John in awe. The warriors made a ring and performed three ceremonial dances, each more amazing than the last. Then they stationed 30 or 40 tall guards around John and served him a feast with enough bread and venison to feed 20 men. He wondered if they wanted to fatten him up so that they could eat him. But he had escaped from being killed—at least for the time being.

The Real Story of Powhatan and Pocahontas

Several days later, John Smith was escorted on a winding river journey past many Indian towns along the Rappahannock and Potomac Rivers. In one town, seven priests in snake skin, weasel pelts, paint, and feathers danced for three days to figure out if their prisoner was good or evil. At the end of the journey, John was delivered to the mighty emperor Powhatan. This ruler who controlled 32 tribes was the finest hunter, most fearsome warrior, and most cunning leader in all Virginia.

As the travelers entered Werowocomoco, the royal court, more than 200 grim warriors lined their way and glared at John as if he were a monster. Tall and ancient, majestic and fierce, Powhatan reclined inside his lodge. Enormous chains of pearls hung round his neck, and he wore a huge, elegant robe made of raccoon skins with their ringed tails hanging down. At his head and feet sat two young women, and along each side wall were two rows of men and women with their heads and shoulders painted blood red.

As John entered the lodge, everyone let out a deafening yell of welcome. One queen offered him water for washing his hands, and another brought a bunch of feathers to dry them. Then a fabulous feast was served. John knew he had to seem calm and fearless. Otherwise, this could be his last meal.

Powhatan demanded to hear why the Englishmen were living in his territory. Afraid that Powhatan would kill any permanent settlers, John made up a story. He told Powhatan that the English had lost a battle

with Spanish ships, were driven up the Chesapeake Bay by bad weather, and landed to get fresh water and repair their boat.

Then why were John Smith and his men exploring rivers so far upstream, Powhatan wanted to know. Thinking fast, John replied that an Englishman had been killed by Powhatan's enemies, the Monacans, who lived in that direction. The explorers wished to avenge his death.

Powhatan could make up good stories, too. He claimed that there was a great salt sea farther up the river beyond some waterfalls. He also told of other men dressed like Englishmen who had come in ships like theirs. (Maybe this was partly true.) The two clever men sparred with words about the warships of England's king, John's amazing compass, and fearsome tribes of Indian cannibals carrying battle axes.

Powhatan then talked to his advisors at great length. Finally, he decided exactly what to do with John Smith.

John Smith was doomed to die. Two big flat stones were placed upon the ground. As many Indians as could lay their hands on him grabbed John by the arms, shoved his head onto the stones, and raised their clubs to beat out his brains. Had John's luck run out? This time, escape seemed impossible.

Just then, a pretty little girl about ten or eleven years old began to plead with Powhatan to spare John's life. Her name was Pocahontas. Even though she was Powhatan's most beloved daughter, on this serious occasion, he ignored every word she said.

In return, Pocahontas ignored the warriors' clubs. She hugged John Smith's head and put her own head on top of his. That's when Powhatan decided to spare John's life. He had escaped from death once again!

Two days later, John was seated alone inside a great house. A terrifying wail arose, and there stood Powhatan all painted black, looking more like a devil than a man. Beside him stood 200 warriors who were painted black too. The clever emperor declared that he and John were now friends. John should go to Jamestown and send him some cannons and a grindstone. In exchange, John would be as beloved as his own son and was now chief of a land on the York River.

John Smith was free! Powhatan sent him to Jamestown with 12 warriors and gifts of food for the colonists. John treated the warriors well, but he was no fool. He knew that sending cannons to Powhatan would be a deadly mistake. The cannons he showed to the Indians weighed three or four thousand pounds apiece. John fired one cannon at a huge tree loaded with icicles, and the ice and branches tumbled down with an enormous crash, terrifying the Indians. Their leader declared that the cannons were too heavy to move. John sent them home with plenty of other gifts—but no weapons.

Powhatan would eventually order his men to try trading, stealing, ambush, and every other trick in the book to get hold of English weapons. John would always trade with the Indians, but never for his cannons or muskets or ammunition or swords. Time after time, this firm stand helped the colonists escape from grave danger.

1608
Vexations & Explorations

VIRGINIA

Smith's Falls
Tockwough
Delaware Bay
Bolus River
Cuskarawook
Patowomek
Potomac River
Rappahannock River
Patuxent River
Richard's Cliffs
Limbo Island
Wighcocomoco
Smith Island
Pt. Ployer
Chesapeake Bay
Stingray Isle
Powhatan River (James River)
Powhatan
Oropax
Pamaunkee
Park River
Werowocomoco
Chickahominy River
Paspahegh
JAMESTOWN
Pamunkey River (James River)
Kecoughtan
Accomack
Cape Charles
Smith Island
CAPE HENRY
ATLANTIC OCEAN

⊙ Indian village
······· 1st voyage
- - - - 2nd voyage

Winter and Spring, 1608
(Age 28)

When John returned to Jamestown, only about 40 colonists were still alive! Some gentlemen were just about to leave the rest behind and sail to England, but John stopped them. In return, they tried to have him hanged. John escaped death once again that very night when a supply ship returned from England and the ship's captain, Christopher Newport, stopped the hanging.

Three days later, Jamestown burned to the ground. If it hadn't been for John's union with Powhatan, everyone would have starved. John's young friend Pocahontas came with other Indians bearing gifts of food from Powhatan.

The ship's captain had brought orders from London to send back gold, or else! Instead of building houses and planting crops, he ordered the men to hunt for gold. John insisted they were wasting valuable time. He was right; no gold was ever found.

Summer 1608

On June 2, John Smith led his first of two explorations of the Chesapeake Bay and the rivers feeding into it. There were adventures a-plenty. Terrifying storms destroyed a sail, and they had to replace it with their shirts. John befriended many Indians, even some who were hostile at first.

The explorers would have given two barrels of gold for one barrel of clean drinking water. On the eastern shore, they finally found some in a pond that was hotter than a bath.

Under cliffs and waterfalls, the men found clay that was bright red, white, or sparkly like gold and silver. Wolves, bears, and other wild beasts seemed to lurk behind every tree.

The reeds in one river were so full of fish that the men grabbed their swords and speared more than they could ever eat. Just then, a stingray's poison tail pierced John's wrist. His hand, arm, and shoulder got so swollen that everyone thought he would die. Once the pain began to go away, he ate the stingray for revenge.

Escapes Five through Ten
John Escapes from Indian Attacks Six Times

John Smith soon set out on his second voyage of exploration. Besides making maps and finding new resources, he also wanted to trade with the Indians. But it was a sure bet that if John's small crew looked weak, they'd be attacked. He would have to come up with some very clever tricks to escape from danger, and he did.

John's fifth escape began as eight of his twelve men lay deathly ill in the bottom of their boat. These sailors had recently arrived from

England and were having a terrible time getting used to Virginia's food and water. Just then, seven or eight canoes full of mighty Massawomeke raiders sped their way, determined to attack. How could John ever escape with only four men left to fight?

Quickly, the sick explorers hid under a tarp while John stuck every hat he could find onto sticks and charged straight toward the Indians. The Massawomekes thought John's boat was full of soldiers. They spun around and fled, but John chased them down. To their great surprise, he didn't shoot; he gave them bells and offered to trade instead. The Massawomekes thought John's boat was too strong to attack. And they had never seen such amazing trade goods. Could he exchange them for a boatload of their bear meat, fish, furs, clubs, shields, bows, and arrows? Of course!

What about the sixth escape? As the explorers entered Tockwough territory, a fleet of Tockwough warriors armed to the teeth surrounded John's boat. Was escape impossible? Not to John. Fearlessly, he called out a friendly greeting. Then he held up the bows and arrows he had just gotten in trade and pretended he had won them in a battle with the Massawomekes, who were the Tockwough's worst enemies. They were so impressed that instead of fighting, they invited the explorers to a fine feast, gave them many gifts, and sang in honor of their "victory." John Smith had escaped again.

On to escape number seven. The Massawomeke shields were so strong they could stop every arrow. The explorers tied several shields to the front of his boat, and it's a good thing they did. While the crew was exploring the Rappahannock River, a few Rappahannock Indians urged John to come up a small creek to trade. It was a trap. As John's boat came near, hundreds of warriors hiding in the forest shot off a torrent of arrows. The Massawomeke shields stopped every one. John's men fired several muskets at once through the spaces between the shields, and the Rappahannocks fled.

What happened the eighth time? John had his men put shields all the way around the boat. The next morning, strange little bushes started popping up along the water's edge, and showers of arrows began to rain down on the explorers. Safe behind their new shields, John's men fired back into the "bushes," which disappeared as mysteriously as they had come. Once their boat was far away, the bushes turned into dancing Rappahannock Indians. Thanks to the shields, John and his men had escaped scott-free.

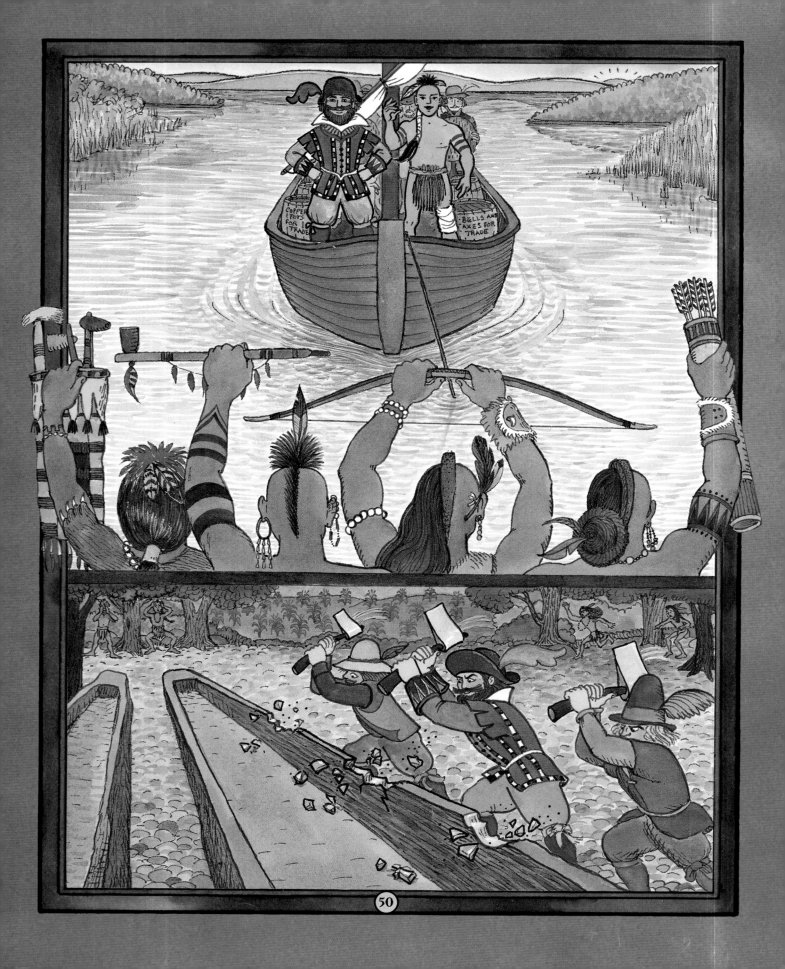

The ninth escape! John's crew was ashore without their weapons when a hundred nimble Hasinninga Indians began shooting at them from the treetops. They thought John had come from the underworld to steal their country. Whooping loudly to sound like lots of warriors, an Indian friend of John's named Mosco started shooting at the attackers. He brought the crew their weapons, and together they drove away the Hasinningas. The fleeing warriors left behind a man named Amoroleck, who had been hit in the knee. John took the injured man on board, told his surgeon to dress the wound, and sailed away. But Indians kept firing at his boat all night.

At dawn, John anchored in a broad bay out of reach of the arrows. Boldly, he removed the shields protecting the boat and ordered his armed men to stand in plain sight with Amoroleck. The wounded Indian told his tribe that John's men were good guys who would free him if they were friendly. Besides, the explorers were protected by magic and couldn't be harmed anyway. Then John gave gifts to the Indians, and their four chiefs—now John's new friends—gave him all the bows, arrows, pipes, and tobacco bags he would ever need.

The tenth escape came after John offered to trade with several Nandsamund Indians. They led the explorers up a narrow river—and into another ambush. When John's men fired back, the Indians ran away. John seized their canoes and started chopping them up. Canoes were so hard to build that the frantic Indians offered John all their kings' weapons, a huge chain of pearls, and 400 baskets of corn to stop the destruction. Not only had John escaped again, but he could feed everyone in Jamestown too.

NEW FRANCE
NEW ENGLAND

MAINE

Pembrocks Bay (Penobscot Bay)

River Forth (Kennebec River)

Mount Battie
Mecaddacut (Camden)

Hoghton Ils (Isle de Haut)

Pemaquid

Back Bay of Portland
Point Kent (Cape Elizabeth)

7

Barty Ils. (Monhegan Island)

6

Snodoun Hill (Mt. Agamenticus)

Cape Davies (Cape Neddick, Savage Rock)

ENGLAND

Smiths Iles

NEW HAMPSHIRE

Agawam (Ipswich)

Cape Tragabigzanda (Cape Ann)

Naumkeag (Salem)

Atlantic Ocean

MASSACHUSETTS

Quonahassit Harbor (Massachusetts Bay)

The River Charles

Accomack (Plymouth)

Milford Haven (Provincetown Harbor)

Cape James (Cape Cod)

Stuards Bay (Cape Cod Bay)

Chawum

CONNECTICUT

RHODE ISLAND

Isle of Nauset

ENGLAND
4 5

NEW ENGLAND
1 2 3

VIRGINIA COLONY

The places John Smith explored had several names over the years. This map shows the names and spellings that John Smith used most often. Other names, including some modern ones, are shown in parentheses. Modern borders and state names are shown in blue for reference.

September 1608 to December 1609 (Ages 28 and 29)

John was elected president of Jamestown. He was the fairest, most successful leader it would ever have. Since so many gentlemen thought work was beneath their dignity, John proclaimed, "He that will not work shall not eat."
The tactic succeeded. Jamestown thrived as never before.

While returning from a river voyage, John dozed with his gunpowder bag on his lap. A spark—possibly from someone's pipe—landed on the bag. It exploded, burning John horribly. Forced to return to England, he left behind a well-supplied colony of 500 healthy people, more than 60 hogs, and 500 chickens.

Six months later, only 60 people were still alive. There was nothing to eat but roots, acorns, and the skins of dead horses. There were even reports of cannibalism. And Pocahontas was told (incorrectly) that her friend John Smith was dead.

1610–1612 (Ages 30–32)

John tried to return to Virginia, but since he wouldn't look for gold or kowtow to wealthy noblemen, all of his requests were turned down.

Some friends from Jamestown came back to England and worked with John Smith to write the story of the colony in a book called A Map of Virginia. John also wrote a 149-page description of the Virginia Indians' way of life.

March to August, 1614 (Age 34)

John was given two ships with a crew of 49 men and boys and was sent to northeastern America to bring back gold, copper, and whales.

There was no gold or copper, and the men couldn't catch any whales. But John found something better: 25 excellent harbors and an awesome abundance of forests, furs, fowl, fish, fruits, farmland, and fresh air. He befriended the Indians and made a fabulous map that can be used to follow his route even now.

He named the area New England, and so it is called to this very day.

John Has Terrible Luck at Sea

I t was hard, but John finally raised enough money for a
second trip to New England. In March 1615, he and 16 excited
colonists set out from Plymouth, England, in two ships.
Almost right away, they found themselves in the middle of a
ferocious storm. All three masts on John's ship broke away and were
swept out to sea. So much water poured through his leaky hull that
the sailors had all they could do to keep pumping it out.

Once the crew rigged up a new mast, the vessel sloshed its way
back to Plymouth. But that didn't stop John for a minute. On June
24, 1615, he and 30 men headed back out to sea in a smaller kind of
ship called a bark.

This time John had no luck at all. Pirates ruled the seas in those
days, and even though his bark wasn't carrying any gold, spices, silk,
or other valuable booty, it was stopped three times by well-armed
pirate ships over twice its size. John's terrified crew begged him to
surrender. They complained that they were hired to fish, not to
fight. Naturally, John swore he'd explode his ship with its own
powder if his men wouldn't defend themselves. One way or another,
the ship managed to escape from the pirates every time.

Just one day after the third attack, four huge French war ships surrounded John Smith's little bark. Then a French captain, who claimed he was policing the ocean in the name of his king, seized John's boat, its crew, its weapons, and all of the supplies that were necessary for setting up the new colony. These Frenchmen had turned out to be pirates just like all the rest.

John's bark was freed a few days later, so he went aboard a ship from the French fleet to gather up his supplies. But the shipmaster back on John's boat had decided he was fed up with fighting pirates. He plotted a mutiny.

When John was ready to return to his ship, the shipmaster lied that a rowboat they usually used for taking passengers back and forth couldn't come because it had split apart. Most of the colonists still wanted to go to America with John Smith. But that night, the mutineers snuck away with John's ship and everyone on it. They sailed straight back to England. Meanwhile, John was trapped on board the French ship with nothing but the clothes on his back.

What could he do? John kept himself busy by writing a new book called *A Description of New England*. The pirates kept busy too by pillaging lots of other ships from many countries. Since Spain was England's worst enemy, John helped out the pirates when Spanish ships were attacked. He was even promised a part of the loot. Did he get his fair share? No. Was he set free? Of course not!

Whenever the ships reached land, the French captain locked John up on board because the men were afraid he might tell someone they were pirates. Two French captains even decided to send John to prison on false charges unless he signed a paper swearing that the French ships were innocent of piracy.

John didn't like this situation one bit. On a very stormy night near the end of October, he wrapped up his new book with great care and secretly slipped overboard in the ship's lifeboat. He had no oars, and the only thing he could use for rowing was a short spear. Swept out to sea and back by the tides, John rowed and bailed and rowed and bailed until he was nearly drowned and half dead from cold and hunger.

Finally a big wave drove John's boat aground on a muddy island, where some bird hunters found him the next morning. The French ship was wrecked by the storm, and its captain and 15 members of the crew were drowned. But John Smith had escaped again!

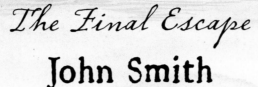

The Final Escape
John Smith
Escapes Obscurity

John was penniless when he reached London in 1615, but he
still had his map and the manuscript for *A Description of
New England*. The book explained why lumber, fish, furs,
and freedom were riches worth far more than gold, and it
stirred up great excitement about America. But every attempt Smith
made to return was jinxed.

In 1617, vicious storms delayed his ships for three months until it was too
late in the season to travel. In 1618, he asked England's Lord Chancellor,
Sir Francis Bacon, to sponsor another trip. His plea was ignored.

When the group later called the Pilgrims wanted to find freedom
of religion in America, John offered to lead their new colony. No
thank you. They took along John's wonderful maps and books instead.

Back in Virginia, colonists and Indians had long been fighting each
other. The English thought it was their right to expand their settle-
ment beyond Jamestown; the Indians strongly disagreed. On March 22,

1622, Opechancanough organized several attacks against colonists living outside of Jamestown. Some 347 English were killed. (There is no record of the number of Indians killed by colonists.) Smith asked the London Council to send him and 100 soldiers to Virginia to teach the colonists to defend themselves. "Too expensive!" the Company decreed. One year later, the colonists' death toll had doubled.

John Smith seemed fated to disappear from history. What could he do? John had always been a man of action, but for his final escape he had to sit still. He escaped obscurity by writing wonderful books telling all about America. Though he could never go there again, he loved the country as if it were his own child. And so it was that his books gave birth to the Great American Dream of a better life on these shores. His ideas have made him a hero to this very day.

61

A Note from the Author

Why haven't we heard more about John Smith's heroic deeds? In early America, he was almost as well loved as George Washington himself. Every school child knew all about him. But then came the Civil War.

When the southern states, including Virginia, seceded from the Union, northern historian Henry Adams decided to undermine the reputation of the South's greatest hero. He wrote a piece of war propaganda in which he claimed that John Smith was a liar and a braggart whose writings were full of phony adventures starring himself as hero. Adams also tried to blacken the reputations of Pocahontas and all of her descendants. The trick worked. Smith went out of favor and stayed that way for a very long time.

Even so, all was not lost. During the past 50 years, there has been renewed interest in John Smith among such highly respected scholars as Philip L. Barbour, J. A. Leo Lemay, David A. Price, Bradford Smith, and Laura Polyani Striker. These historians have compared Smith's works to the entire array of writing by Smith's friends, his enemies, war chroniclers, and Turkish battle reporters, and each of them confirms the basic accuracy of Smith's accounts.

Some scholars note that Smith's tales are told only from a Western European, Protestant point of view or that he may have embroidered his escapades (a common practice at the time). All agree that today's popular love stories about John Smith and Pocahontas are false. The young Indian was never Smith's sweetheart; she was only a little girl at the time. Lemay argues persuasively that Pocahontas did cover Smith's head with her own to save his life. Lemay and other scholars suggest that the rescue might have been a ceremony in which Smith "died" and was "reborn" as a member of the tribe. Some other historians believe that the event never happened. We may never know for sure.

This book is closely based on John Smith's own writings. You might have noticed that Smith didn't always present a well-rounded view of his Catholic, Turkic, Indian, or other opponents. They were his enemies even when he respected them, and if any of them were telling the story, you can bet they would be the good guys, and John and the English (or Austrians, etc.) would be the bad guys. All stories—even nonfiction ones—are told from someone's point of view.

And why is John Smith one of America's greatest heroes? There are plenty of reasons. Jamestown, England's first permanent colony in America, would never have survived without him. He was a great leader: tough, honest, brave, practical, and fair. He respected the Indians and never tried to destroy them the way so many Europeans did. He worked hard and would go to any length to be sure that everyone had enough to eat. But most important of all, John Smith loved America and all its possibilities. He spent most of his life trying to make this beautiful world into a place where class rank didn't matter and where anyone willing to work hard could become a success. That sounds like a hero to me.

About the Illustrations

Yes, young girls like Pocahontas would have shaved the top part of their heads, and Indian warriors really did wear live snakes in their ears. I researched hundreds of paintings, engravings, and book illustrations from John Smith's era to try to make sure that every Turkish warrior, French pirate ship, Indian tattoo, and other detail I drew would be as accurate as possible. I scrutinized the pictures in John Smith's own books, as well as photos of artifacts found in Jamestown and detailed descriptions of the Indians made by Smith and other colonists. My pictures of Smith's face after he grew up are based on the portrait engraved on his map of New England.

Bibliography

Barbour, Philip L. *The Three Worlds of Captain John Smith*. Boston: Houghton Mifflin, 1964.

Haile, Edward Wright, editor. *Jamestown Narratives: Eyewitness Accounts of the Virginia Colony*. Champlain, Virginia: RoundHouse, 1998.

Lankford, John, editor. *Captain John Smith's America: Selections from his Writings*. New York: Harper Torchbooks, 1967.

Kupperman, Karen Ordahl, editor. *Captain John Smith: A Selected Edition of his Writings*. Chapel Hill, North Carolina: University of North Carolina Press, 1988.

Lemay, J. A. Leo. *The American Dream of Captain John Smith*. Charlottesville, Virginia: University Press of Virginia, 1991.

____. *Did Pocahontas Save Captain John Smith?* Athens, Georgia: University of Georgia Press, 1992.

Price, David A. *Love and Hate in Jamestown: John Smith, Pocahontas, and the Heart of a New Nation*. New York: Knopf, 2003.

Smith, Bradford. *Captain John Smith: His Life and Legend*. Philadelphia: Lippincott, 1953.

Smith, John and Philip L. Barbour. *The Complete Works of Captain John Smith, 1580–1631*. Chapel Hill, North Carolina: University of North Carolina Press, 1986.

Index

GREENLAND

NEW
FRANCE

NEWFOUNDLAND

PLYMOUTH COLONY

NOVA SCOTIA

ESCAPES FROM
INDIAN ATTACKS
SIX TIMES
Pp. 46-57

⑨

SAVED BY
A COMPASS
p. 33

⑦ ⑧

VIRGINIA
COLONY

RESCUED BY
POCAHONTAS
p. 40

Florida

Azores

⑩

IMPRISONED
BY PIRATES
p. 58

N

Atlantic
Ocean

Cuba

Hispaniola

Puerto
Rico

CARIBBEAN SEA

Nevis